The Art and Science of Spycraft

Special Edition

The Art and Science of Spycraft
Special Edition

A Field Manual for Everyday Tradecraft

P.J. AGNESS

The Art and Science of Spycraft: Special Edition

Part of the Spycraft Library.

SPECIAL EDITION NOTE

This Special Edition rebuilds the original Spycraft Library book into a fuller P.J. Agness field manual. The earlier material remains where it still carries the cleanest lesson, but the book now has a new working layer: briefing material, doctrine laws, field cards, civilian operations, expanded case files, field workbook pages, drills, a lexicon, a challenge sequence, and a final field exam.

The goal is not to make spycraft theatrical. The goal is to make it usable. A reader should be able to leave this edition with sharper habits for trust, access, information, timing, position, privacy, and personal security.

The standard remains lawful, practical, and restrained. Spycraft here means awareness, judgment, self-control, relationship skill, and the disciplined management of information in ordinary life.

BRIEFING ROOM: READ THIS FIRST

This is not a book about pretending to be a spy. Pretending is usually loud, fragile, and easy to spot. The useful version of spycraft is quieter. It is the way you enter a room, protect information, read pressure, build trust, notice exits, control your reaction, and leave yourself more than one option.

Most people walk through life giving away position. They answer too much, react too quickly, trust too cheaply, and notice the wrong things. They mistake information for understanding and urgency for importance. The result is familiar: they get pulled by other people's moods, trapped by bad timing, and surprised by patterns that were visible long before the problem became loud.

This manual is built to correct that. The tools are small because real control usually begins small. A name used at the right moment. A pause before an answer. A seat that keeps the entrance in view. A private fact kept private. A question that reveals motive without making the room defensive. None of it looks dramatic. That is why it works.

Read this edition with a field mindset. Do not collect clever ideas. Test behaviors. A principle you practice once becomes a note. A principle you practice for a month becomes part of your operating system. That is the difference between reading spycraft and carrying it.

HOW TO USE THIS BOOK

Do not read this book like trivia. Read it like a working manual. One section should give you one usable behavior. If you cannot test the idea in ordinary life, you have not finished the lesson yet.

The best approach is simple. Read one principle, use the field exercise for a week, and then decide what changed. Did you notice more. Did you leak less information. Did you improve position. Did an interaction become easier because you noticed the other person's motive. That is the test.

You do not need to perform spycraft. In fact, performance is usually the tell. The better habit is quiet integration. Count exits without staring. Learn names without sounding rehearsed. Ask better questions without interrogating people. Protect privacy without turning every conversation into a drama. The ordinary version is the useful version.

The 12 Laws of Everyday Spycraft

These laws are the spine of this edition. They are not slogans for display. They are working rules for ordinary pressure, ordinary people, and ordinary rooms where advantage is usually decided before anyone recognizes a contest has begun.

Law 1: Trust is access.

People open doors for people they trust. That door may be literal, social, professional, emotional, or informational. If you burn trust, you shrink the world around you. If you build it patiently, people tell you more, include you sooner, and forgive small friction faster.

Law 2: Position beats force.

Better position reduces the need for confrontation. A person who has exits, information, allies, timing, and calm often needs less volume and less force. Before trying to win, improve position.

Law 3: Attention is a weapon.

Where attention goes, judgment follows. If someone can capture your attention, they can often steer your choices. Guard your attention like a limited resource because it is one.

LAW 4: THE ROOM ALWAYS TALKS.

Every environment gives off signals.
Layout, mood, noise, crowd flow, staff
behavior, exits, bottlenecks, and small
deviations all speak before people do.
The person who hears the room early moves
earlier.

LAW 5: CALM IS CONCEALMENT.

Stress leaks information. It changes
voice, pace, posture, timing, and
judgment. Calm does not make you
invisible, but it gives away less and
buys you time to choose the next move.

LAW 6: NAMES TURN STRANGERS INTO PEOPLE.

A name changes the social field. It
personalizes the interaction, lowers
friction, and creates a small thread of
recognition. Used honestly, names build
warmth faster than clever lines.

LAW 7: MOTIVE MOVES THE MACHINE.

People act from pressure, desire, fear,
pride, love, money, convenience,
ideology, ego, and loss. Do not stop at
what someone says. Look for what moves
them.

LAW 8: PRIVACY IS A DISCIPLINE.

Most leaks are voluntary. People
surrender private information because
silence feels awkward, convenience feels
harmless, or approval feels good. Keep

what belongs to you. Answer only what
serves the moment.

LAW 9: PATTERNS ARE MAPS.

Routine creates efficiency, but it also
creates predictability. Learn the
patterns around you. Protect your own. A
pattern noticed early often reveals
motive, pressure, or risk before the
event announces itself.

LAW 10: TIMING CHANGES THE MEANING OF EVERY MOVE.

The same words can sound helpful, weak,
aggressive, or wise depending on timing.
Speak too early and you expose need.
Speak too late and you surrender ground.
Wait long enough to see the room clearly.

LAW 11: THE BORING ANSWER IS OFTEN THE STRONGEST.

Good tradecraft rarely looks clever. It
looks like reliability, restraint, simple
planning, clean exits, and ordinary
behavior that does not attract extra
attention.

LAW 12: FREEDOM OF ACTION IS THE PRIZE.

The point is not control for its own
sake. The point is options. If a habit
gives you more lawful choices, clearer
judgment, and cleaner exits, it belongs
in your kit.

FIELD CARD: THE 12-LAW CHECK

Before a hard conversation, unfamiliar place, or pressured decision, ask which law matters most right now. Do you need trust, position, attention control, privacy, timing, or freedom of action. One clean answer will often simplify the next move.

P.J.'s Rules for Not Looking Like a Try-Hard Spy Nerd

The fastest way to ruin useful tradecraft is to perform it. Do not stare at people like you are scanning a suspect board. Do not dress like a movie assassin. Do not turn every conversation into an interrogation. If the method makes ordinary people uncomfortable before it makes you useful, the method is being used badly.

Rule one: look normal. Normal is underrated camouflage. The best tradecraft fits the room so cleanly that nobody knows you are doing anything except being present, polite, and calm.

Rule two: do not overuse jargon. The language is useful for teaching, but ordinary life does not need to hear you announce MICE, SDR, Glomar, or HUMINT every time you notice something. Keep the concept inside your head and let your behavior carry the lesson.

Rule three: awareness is not staring.
Awareness is a quick scan, a quiet
update, and a return to normal social
behavior. If your security habits make
you look unstable, you have created a new
problem.

Rule four: questions should feel human.
Ask because you are listening, not
because you are extracting. Curiosity
works when the other person feels seen.
It fails when they feel processed.

Rule five: mystery is not a
personality. You do not need to act
cryptic. Speak clearly, answer cleanly,
and keep private things private without
making privacy into theater.

Rule six: never let the tool become the
identity. Spycraft should make you
steadier, warmer when warmth is useful,
quieter when quiet is useful, and harder
to push around. If it makes you arrogant,
paranoid, or socially strange, strip it
back to basics.

FIELD EXERCISE: THE NORMALCY TEST

Use one skill today so quietly that
nobody would know it was a skill. Count
exits, learn a name, hold back an
unnecessary detail, or pause before
answering. The cleaner it looks, the
better the rep.

THE SPYCRAFT OPERATING SYSTEM

The chain behind this book is simple: trust creates access, access produces information, information improves timing, timing improves position, position expands options, and options make control possible.

This is the operating system. If trust fails, access shrinks. If access shrinks, information thins. If information thins, timing gets sloppy. If timing gets sloppy, position weakens. If position weakens, options narrow. Once options narrow, other people and events begin controlling the frame.

Most people try to force outcomes at the end of the chain. They demand control before they have position, timing, information, access, or trust. That is why their effort feels loud and unstable. Tradecraft works in the opposite direction. Build the earlier links and the later links become easier to hold.

FIELD CARD: THE CHAIN

- Trust creates access.
- Access produces information.
- Information improves timing.
- Timing improves position.
- Position expands options.
- Options make control possible.

FIELD EXERCISE: THE CHAIN AUDIT

Choose one real problem and identify the earliest weak link in the chain. Improve that link before forcing a solution downstream.

INFORMATION HIERARCHY:

Most people drown in data because they treat all information as equal. It is not. Some information is decorative. Some is emotional. Some is delayed. Some is actionable. Tradecraft begins when you separate noise from signal and signal from decision.

Ask four questions. What do I know. What do I only think I know. What matters right now. What can wait. That short audit keeps rumor from outrunning judgment and keeps urgency attached to the facts that can actually change your next move.

The practical advantage is calm. When you rank information correctly, you stop reacting to every headline, every comment, and every stray clue. You preserve attention for the details that change position, risk, timing, or motive. That is how ordinary awareness becomes intelligence.

FIELD CARD: INFORMATION HIERARCHY

- What do I know.

- What do I only think I know.
- What changes risk, timing, motive, or position.
- What can wait.
- What would I do differently if this information were wrong.

FIELD EXERCISE: FOUR QUESTIONS

For one week, when a stressful message, rumor, or headline hits you, write four answers: what I know, what I think I know, what matters now, and what can wait. Watch how much panic disappears when information gets ranked.

CIVILIAN OPERATION: SIGNAL CHECK

You receive a dramatic message from someone you trust. It claims that a situation is urgent, someone is angry, and action is needed now. The ordinary response is to feel the pressure and start moving. The tradecraft response is to slow the information down before it moves you.

Separate the message into three piles: known facts, claims, and emotional weather. The fact may be that a meeting changed, a person complained, or a deadline moved. The claim may be why it happened. The weather is the fear, irritation, or embarrassment wrapped around the facts. Most bad decisions begin when those three piles get mixed together.

Your move is not to distrust everything. Your move is to rank information before acting on it. Ask what would change your next decision and what merely changes your mood. Then answer from the stable facts, not from the fog around them.

POSITION:

Tradecraft is really the management of position. Physical position in a room. Social position in a hierarchy. Informational position in a conversation. Psychological position under pressure. The person with better position usually needs less force.

That is why small advantages matter. Sitting with the door in view, knowing the baseline, entering through a trusted introduction, or holding one useful fact the other side does not know you have. None of those things look dramatic. Together they change what is possible.

When in doubt, improve position before trying to win. Move closer to exits, information, and decision-makers. Move farther from panic, ego, and spectacle. Many problems solve themselves once your position improves.

FIELD CARD: POSITION

- Where am I exposed.
- Where are the exits.
- Who controls access.
- Who controls information.

• What single move would improve my
options.

FIELD EXERCISE: THE POSITION SCAN

In every public room today, identify the
main entrance, the nearest usable exit,
the person who controls the space, and
one place where you would move if the
mood changed. Do it quietly and then
return to normal.

TRUST:

Trust is currency. It is the quiet asset
behind friendships, dates, referrals,
repeat business, and good intelligence. A
person who is trusted gets access that a
clever person without trust never will.

A dishonest car salesman may make quick
money, but he burns the bridge that would
have produced repeat customers and easy
recommendations. An average mechanic who
has earned trust will be praised like a
genius. In ordinary life, trust
multiplies reputation.

HUMINT runs on the same principle.
Human sources do not open up without
trust, and influence does not last
without it. If you want better
information, better relationships, and
better opportunities, become a person
others trust.

FIELD CARD: TRUST

• What have I done that makes me easier to trust.
• What have I done that makes me harder to trust.
• Where have I overpromised.
• What small reliability deposit can I make today.

FIELD EXERCISE: THE RELIABILITY DEPOSIT

Make one small promise you can keep easily, then keep it quickly. Send the update, return the item, arrive when you said you would, or remember the detail someone gave you. Trust grows through small proof.

SHIFTING MINDSETS:

HUMINT is relationship work. Influence begins with attention, not performance. Techniques matter, but they do not do much without the right operating mindset.

The first shift is perspective. Most people react to the slice of reality directly in front of them. The better move is to step back, ask what else is happening, and gather information before acting. A spy wants informational superiority before emotion takes over.

Picture arriving late to lunch and getting an outsized emotional reaction from a friend. A smart person recognizes

the larger picture immediately. The issue
is probably not the lunch. The same habit
applies everywhere else. Before you
react, ask what you are not seeing yet.

The second shift is from internal focus
to external focus. Most people are
trapped in their own heads, worrying
about how they are being received. That
makes them awkward and blind at the same
time.

On a date, in a meeting, or in
conflict, stop trying to manage how you
look. Pay attention instead. Listen to
learn. Ask open questions. Let the other
person talk long enough for you to notice
what matters to them.

This is the irony. People become more
interesting when they stop trying so hard
to seem interesting. A spy gathers
intelligence by listening. Social
confidence works the same way. Get the
larger view, then get out of your own
head.

FIELD EXERCISE: EXTERNAL FOCUS

In your next conversation, stop
monitoring your own performance. Ask two
open questions and listen for motive,
pressure, and emotion. Your job is not to
impress. Your job is to understand.

THE POWER OF NAMES:

It is easy for people to get angry at,
mistreat, or disregard a stranger.

However, once they view someone as a person, an individual, they must deal with them differently. This is the power of a name. Say, for instance, I bump into a person in public, and they get angry. I could say I'm sorry. However, it is more powerful for me to say "That was clumsy of me. I'm P.J." Now I've personalized myself. It changes everything. It's the same if I'm interacting with a server at a restaurant, a customer service representative, or some government bureaucrat. Once I introduce myself, by name, I am no longer just some stranger, a concept, some anonymous jerk that you have to deal with. I have suddenly become a fellow human being. If I don't wish them to know my real name, that's fine. I still give them a fake name. I usually will still give out my real first name. They can have a fake last name if it gets to that, but I do give out my genuine first name, because I'm seeking a genuine connection. Experiment with this. Slip your first name into an interaction as soon as possible. To take it up a notch, ask others their first name and use their name as soon and as often as possible. Go ahead and try it. It's like a Jedi mind trick.

P.J. FIELD NOTE

A name is not magic. It is a small act of personalization. People become more careful with someone who has stopped being anonymous.

FIELD EXERCISE: THE NAME TEST

Use your first name early in three low-risk interactions. Ask for the other person's name when appropriate. Notice whether the interaction becomes warmer, calmer, or more cooperative.

CIVILIAN OPERATION: COFFEE COUNTER

A low-stakes counter interaction is a perfect training ground because nothing dramatic is at stake. You order coffee, food, parts, tickets, or help. The person behind the counter expects to be treated like furniture. You do something different.

Use your first name early if it fits. Ask theirs if the interaction naturally allows it. Then use it once before you leave. Not five times. Not with fake warmth. Once is enough to change the texture of the exchange. The interaction becomes person to person instead of customer to function.

The lesson is not that names are magic. The lesson is that personalization changes access. People are more patient with a person than with a role. The small moment teaches the larger principle.

ENVIRONMENTAL MASTERY:

Master the environment before you ever need it. When you enter a building, count entrances and exits, notice which ones are usable, and know where trouble would most likely come from. Sit where you can see the main entry when you can.

Use posted fire maps and floor plans, but also walk the space. If you are bad with directions, physical familiarity matters more than a diagram. A few minutes of wandering builds better recall than wishful thinking.

Once you know the routes, identify cover and concealment. Concealment hides you. Cover actually stops rounds. Know the difference.

Both are temporary. The point is not to hide forever. The point is to buy time, move intelligently, and get out.

P.J. FIELD NOTE

Awareness is not staring. Staring makes you part of the problem in the room. Good awareness is a quiet inventory you complete while still behaving normally.

FIELD CARD: ENVIRONMENTAL MASTERY

- Where would trouble enter.
- Where would people naturally bottleneck.
- What cover exists.
- What only conceals.
- Where would I move first if the mood changed.

FIELD EXERCISE: THREE EXITS

Before sitting down in three different places, identify three ways out if possible: the obvious exit, the secondary exit, and the ugly exit. The ugly exit is the one you would use only if the normal route failed.

CIVILIAN OPERATION: EXIT SEAT

Walk into a restaurant with one quiet job: choose position before comfort chooses for you. Do not make a performance of it. Scan the entrance, the exits, the staff lane, the restrooms, the bar, and the crowd density. Then sit where you can see the main flow without looking like you are guarding a border checkpoint.

After you sit, name the nearest usable exit and the obstacle between you and it. Is it a table, crowd, kitchen door, stroller, server station, or narrow hallway. Most people do not know what blocks them until they need to move. You are learning that before pressure arrives.

This is not paranoia. It is environmental literacy. The same habit helps in storms, medical emergencies, arguments, fires, and ordinary confusion. Position first. Meal second.

CONTROL:

External control looks impressive, but most of it is borrowed. Titles, offices, uniforms, and authority only work so long as other people keep cooperating. The control that lasts is internal. It is the breath before you answer, the discipline to do the work you said you would do, and the steadiness to stay useful when other people are spinning.

That is why self control sits at the center of tradecraft. A calm person notices more, leaks less, and makes fewer expensive mistakes. If you can govern your attention, your tongue, your temper, and your routines, you carry real control with you. Everything else is theater unless this part is in place.

FIELD CARD: CONTROL

- Can I slow my answer.
- Can I reduce my words.
- Can I keep my face neutral.
- Can I choose the next move instead of reacting to the last insult.

FIELD EXERCISE: THE SLOW ANSWER

When someone pressures you for an immediate reaction, pause for two seconds before answering. Keep your face neutral. Use fewer words than you want to use. Notice how much control lives in the pause.

INTUITION:

Always trust your gut. Human beings rationalize danger away more than almost any animal on earth. We do it because we want to be polite, optimistic, or liked. That habit gets people hurt.

If something feels wrong, treat that feeling as information. It does not mean panic. It means pause, reassess, and create distance when you can. Your instincts are part of your personal protection system. Strengthen them by listening the first time.

FIELD EXERCISE: FIRST SIGNAL LOG

When something feels off, write down the first signal before explaining it away. Later, check whether the signal meant danger, discomfort, or simply uncertainty. This trains instinct without turning it into panic.

CROWDS:

There is no wisdom in a crowd by default. Crowds magnify emotion, reduce judgment, and make otherwise ordinary people do stupid things. Once you are deep inside one, your options shrink fast.

Stay out of the center. If a crowd forms around you, move calmly and quietly toward the edge before the mood changes. Do not panic, do not posture, and do not let yourself get pulled into group behavior.

This matters in protests, emergencies, sales events, and any situation where panic spreads faster than facts. Crowds hoard, trample, riot, and stampede because individuals stop thinking like individuals.

Be your own sheepdog. Keep your judgment when other people lose theirs.

FIELD CARD: CROWDS

• Where is the edge.
• Which direction is the crowd pulling.
• What emotion is spreading.
• Where are employees, exits, or barriers.
• When should I leave before everyone else decides to.

FIELD EXERCISE: EDGE HABIT

At any crowded place this week, choose a position near the edge instead of the center. Identify where the crowd would compress if people surged. The goal is not fear. It is mobility.

CIVILIAN OPERATION: EDGE OF THE ROOM

Go to a busy public place and study the crowd from the edge. The edge matters because it preserves options. From there you can see flow, exits, bottlenecks, mood, and the people who are moving against the rhythm.

Notice who is leading attention. It may be a loud person, an angry person, a performer, a child, a security guard, or a line that has started to fail. Crowds often turn when attention concentrates. The earlier you notice that concentration, the earlier you can move.

The drill is successful when you can
leave before you need to leave. That is
the difference between awareness and
reaction.

THE BONDS:

Spy work is less like an action movie and
more like a dangerous sales job. The real
work is relationships. Intelligence
officers recruit people, earn access, and
build assets.

You can do the same thing in ordinary
life without pretending you are in a
thriller. Learn the name of the person
behind the counter. Ask about their day.
Be useful. Offer a small favor. Ask for a
small favor when appropriate. Reciprocity
bonds people faster than impressive
speeches.

Build those relationships close to
home. The gas station, the restaurant,
the workplace, the neighborhood. In a
crisis or a conflict, helpful people are
force multipliers. Assets do not have to
feel exotic to be valuable.

FIELD EXERCISE: LOCAL ASSET MAP

Identify five people in your normal
routine who could become useful friendly
contacts: a clerk, neighbor, coworker,
bartender, maintenance worker, or
receptionist. Learn one name and make one
small goodwill deposit.

The Motivators:

People move for reasons. MICE is a useful shorthand. Money, ideology, coercion, and ego.

Money is broader than cash. It can mean convenience, access, relief, or opportunity. Ideology is what people believe they are serving. Ego is how they need to see themselves.

Coercion works, but it is unstable and dangerous. It creates resentment, not loyalty.

You do not need to become manipulative to use this framework. You just need to pay attention to what actually moves people.

When you understand motive, your timing improves, your asks get cleaner, and your misreads go down.

FIELD EXERCISE: MOTIVE READ

Choose one person whose behavior recently confused you. Write down what money, ideology, coercion, ego, fear, anger, love, or laziness might explain. Do not accuse. Use the map to sharpen your read.

The Degree:

If you ever need distance between yourself and your real identity, stay close to the truth. Use a name you will

answer to. Keep the backstory only one
degree off from reality. The farther you
drift, the more details you have to
remember and the easier it is to crack
under pressure.

Good cover is not theatrical. It is
consistent.

FIELD EXERCISE: ONE DEGREE COVER

Create a harmless privacy answer for a
question you dislike. Keep it close to
truth, short, and boring. Practice saying
it without overexplaining.

DISGUISE:

Good disguise is not costume first. It is
behavior first. Walk, posture, pace,
voice, footwear, and environmental fit
matter as much as clothes.

Keep it simple. Change the silhouette,
change the color, change the energy, and
match the setting. Practical camouflage
is about looking like you belong, not
looking clever.

FIELD EXERCISE: SILHOUETTE CHANGE

Change one low-stakes identification cue:
jacket, hat, bag, posture, walking pace,
or color profile. Notice which cues
change recognition and which ones do not.

CAT-AND-MOUSE:

If you think you are being watched, verify before you panic. A simple SDR works because repeated unusual movements are hard to explain away. Three right turns, doubling back in a store, abrupt pauses, and other clean deviations can make a follower stand out.

Do not create a chase, do not run home, and do not isolate yourself. Once you are confident you are being followed, get around employees, security, police, or other people who can help.

FIELD EXERCISE: PATTERN BREAK

In a safe public setting, make one clean deviation from your path: stop, reverse direction, browse, or change aisles. Notice who continues naturally and who repeats the change.

THE BUMP:

A bump is a staged accidental meeting with someone you have already researched. Used well, it lets you arrive prepared while appearing spontaneous.

The point is not to show off what you know. The point is to use prior information to make the interaction feel easy, familiar, and well timed.

FIELD EXERCISE: PREPARED CASUAL

Before meeting someone, learn one harmless preference or interest. Use it only if it arises naturally. The win is making the conversation easier, not proving you researched them.

THE DROP:

A dead drop is a discreet exchange without direct contact. The principle matters even more than the classic spy imagery. The location must be obvious to both parties, quick to use, and natural enough to avoid attention.

In ordinary life, the lesson is simple. Good handoffs are quiet, preplanned, and boring.

FIELD EXERCISE: CLEAN HANDOFF

Plan one ordinary handoff so it requires no extra conversation: where, when, what object, and what confirmation. Good logistics should feel boring.

THE BRUSH:

A brush pass is the contact version of the same idea. Brief contact, minimal attention, and a transfer that looks ordinary. The cleaner it looks, the better it works.

FIELD EXERCISE: LOW ATTENTION TRANSFER

Practice making a normal exchange smoother: keys, paperwork, a receipt, a note, or a borrowed item. Minimize drama, extra words, and visible confusion.

THE PATTERN:

Routine is efficient, but it also makes you easy to study. Change departure times, routes, and habits enough that no one can map your life at a glance. Predictability is comfort for you and opportunity for someone else.

FIELD EXERCISE: ROUTINE SHAKE

Change one predictable routine this week: route, departure time, parking spot, lunch location, or errand order. Keep it reasonable. The goal is to stop being easily mapped.

CIVILIAN OPERATION: PATTERN BREAK

Pick one routine you repeat without thinking: the same parking spot, the same route, the same posting time, the same place you leave keys, the same after-work stop. Do not blow up your life. Change one small element for one week.

The value is twofold. First, you become less easy to map. Second, you learn which parts of your routine are convenience and which parts are dependency. A routine you can alter remains a tool. A routine you cannot alter has started managing you.

Pattern breaking should make you freer, not frantic. If the change adds chaos without improving options, choose a cleaner change.

OPEN-SOURCES:

OSINT is the civilian's intelligence discipline. Public information, properly gathered and interpreted, gives ordinary people an advantage previous generations never had.

Do not get lost collecting everything. Use open sources to answer specific questions, verify what you think you know, and make better decisions. The tool matters less than the discipline.

FIELD EXERCISE: QUESTION FIRST

Before searching, write the exact question you need answered. Gather only what helps answer it. Stop when the answer is good enough for the decision.

BASELINING:

Every person and every environment has a baseline. The useful question is not whether something looks strange in the abstract. The question is whether it is strange for that person, that room, or that moment. A talkative friend going quiet, a careful coworker getting sloppy, or a cheerful crowd with one angry outlier all deserve attention because they break pattern.

Baselining matters for both safety and deception detection. Nervous behavior does not prove a lie if the person is normally nervous. Restlessness only means more when it departs from their usual rhythm. Watch enough to learn what normal looks like, then trust the deviation when it appears. Small perception, applied consistently, creates a large advantage.

FIELD EXERCISE: NORMAL BEFORE STRANGE

Pick one familiar person or place. For three days, observe what normal looks like before judging deviations. Baseline first, interpret second.

SIMPLE SABOTAGE:

The OSS understood something modern offices prove every day. An organization can be crippled without explosions, just through delay, confusion, misplaced priorities, needless meetings, and procedural drag.

That is the enduring lesson of simple sabotage. Systems break when people insist on channels over results, reward the incompetent, multiply approvals, reopen settled decisions, and bury urgent work under ceremony.

You do not need the destructive examples to grasp the value of the lesson. Learn to spot friction, artificial delay, and morale killing behavior. If you lead people, remove it. If you are surrounded by it, at least recognize what it is.

This section is here as history and pattern recognition, not as a how to manual for doing stupid things.

FIELD EXERCISE: FRICTION HUNT

Find one source of needless delay in your work or home life. Remove one approval, one repeated decision, one unclear instruction, or one useless meeting from your personal system.

MIRRORING:

Mirroring builds trust when it is subtle. Match energy, pace, and body language without becoming a parody. The goal is not mimicry. The goal is to signal safety, similarity, and understanding.

Done badly, it feels fake. Done well, it makes people feel seen.

FIELD EXERCISE: PACE MATCH

In a low-stakes conversation, match only pace and volume. Do not copy gestures. Notice whether the other person relaxes when your rhythm fits theirs.

The C Words:

The best fictional spies share three traits. Calm, cool, and confident. None of that requires theatrics. It mostly requires slower reactions, fewer wasted words, and better emotional control.

Silence helps. Deliberate speech helps. Refusing to take every insult at face value helps. Confidence is often a matter of pace.

Criminals hunt soft targets. You do not have to look like a fighter to look like a harder decision.

Field Exercise: Quiet Confidence

For one day, reduce filler words, slow your first sentence, and stop explaining after the answer is complete. Confidence often sounds like enough.

Combatives:

Self-defense is not about pretty technique. It is about protecting life, damaging vulnerable targets if you must, and getting out. Simplicity beats flair.

Use durable tools, not fragile ones. Palms, elbows, knees, and the head used correctly are sturdier than fists. Attack soft targets, create an opening, and escape.

The goal is not to win a cinematic fight. The goal is to survive the real one.

FIELD EXERCISE: EXIT BEFORE TECHNIQUE

In three public places, ask where you would move before any physical problem became physical. The first self-defense technique is often leaving early.

WEAPONS:

Avoid unarmed combat when you can. Anything that creates distance, buys time, blocks damage, or distracts an attacker may be more useful than empty hands.

Think in categories. Offensive tools, defensive tools, and distraction tools. Many ordinary objects can serve more than one role.

Improvisation matters more than gear. The best weapon is often the object you can reach first and use decisively.

FIELD EXERCISE: OBJECT CATEGORIES

Look around one room and sort reachable objects into defensive, distraction, and distance tools. Do not fantasize. Think about what buys time and space.

Catching Canaries:

Loose lips destroy privacy. The canary trap solves that problem by giving different people slightly different versions of the same information. When something leaks, the leak identifies itself.

The principle is simple and useful well beyond espionage. If something matters, control distribution and make the trail traceable.

FIELD EXERCISE: TRACEABLE DETAIL

Share harmless but slightly different versions of a non-sensitive detail with two people. Notice how quickly small differences make a trail visible.

The Gambit:

You cannot foresee every outcome, but you can train yourself to look for the advantage inside the outcome you got. That is the practical version of the Xanatos Gambit.

Do not waste a setback by treating it as pure loss. Ask what it teaches, what it redirects, and what it spared you.

FIELD EXERCISE: SALVAGE THE SETBACK

When something goes wrong this week, write down one advantage hidden inside

the result: information gained, bad
option removed, timing improved, or
weakness exposed.

ESCAPE:

Always have an escape plan. Count exits,
notice which ones actually work, and
position yourself with entrances in view
when you can.

Escape planning is not paranoia. It is
basic environmental literacy. Know how
danger would enter, know how you would
leave, and do not wait to think about it
after something starts.

FIELD EXERCISE: LEAVE EARLY RULE

Choose one event or environment where you
will leave before fatigue, alcohol, crowd
mood, or conflict makes leaving harder.
Escape improves when you do it before the
alarm bell.

THE BANK:

In HUMINT, relationships are a form of
capital. Every favor, every kept
confidence, every honest conversation
adds to the account. That reserve becomes
useful the moment you need information,
cover, help, or a good word.

FIELD EXERCISE: RELATIONSHIP DEPOSIT

Make one no-strings-attached deposit into a useful relationship: useful information, a favor, a thank you, a referral, or a kept confidence.

AGENTS:

Intelligence officers are not spies in the Hollywood sense. Their real job is to recruit people who already have access, motive, or placement. Those people become agents. In ordinary life, the same principle applies. You do not always solve a problem by confronting it directly. Sometimes you solve it by recruiting the right people to care.

FIELD EXERCISE: ACCESS MAP

Choose one problem and list the people with access to information, permission, tools, or influence. The direct route is not always the cleanest route.

PROPAGANDA:

Propaganda is not just an opinion you dislike. It is messaging designed to shape feeling over time so that later choices feel natural. The most effective propaganda does not order people around. It changes the emotional climate, the assumptions, and the categories people use before they ever think they are making a decision.

The practical defense is simple. Ask how the message wants you to feel, what conclusion it is preparing you to accept, and whose interests it serves. Pay attention to repetition, moral framing, selective outrage, and the stories that keep showing up with different names attached. Once you see the emotional architecture, the spell weakens.

The offensive lesson is more restrained. Reputation, rumor, and example all influence the people around you. If something false is spreading, counter it through visible behavior and consistent framing. If you want to move a group, emotion usually arrives before argument. Recognize propaganda, resist crude versions of it, and understand how narrative and feeling travel together.

P.J. FIELD NOTE

The cleanest defense is not outrage. Outrage is often the delivery system. Slow down and ask what feeling the message is trying to install before it asks you to believe anything.

FIELD EXERCISE: FEELING FIRST

Before reacting to a persuasive message, name the feeling it wants from you. Fear, disgust, pride, guilt, urgency, or belonging. Then decide whether the conclusion still holds.

THE KISS:

Keep it simple, stupid. The principle survives because it is right. Complex plans fail in complex ways. Simple plans are easier to execute, easier to remember, and easier to adapt when something changes.

That is the spirit of this book and of the library around it. Tradecraft should make life clearer, not more theatrical. Learn the principle, test it in ordinary life, keep what proves durable, and drop what only sounds clever on paper.

FIELD EXERCISE: SIMPLIFY THE PLAN

Take one plan you are overcomplicating and reduce it to the next three physical actions. If you cannot do that, you do not have a plan yet.

ASSESSMENT:

Good decisions start with assessment. Acronyms help people remember process, but the underlying habit is older and simpler than any acronym. Look first. Orient yourself. Decide from what is actually in front of you, not from panic, pride, or wishful thinking.

In fast situations, the cleanest question is often the best one. What can hurt me the quickest. That question clears away lesser worries and helps you

prioritize the danger that matters now,
not the inconvenience you can solve
later.

Assessment is not a one-time event. It
is a loop. Conditions change, information
arrives, and what was true ten seconds
ago may no longer be true. Reassess as
you move.

The opposite danger is paralysis.
Overthinking under pressure can be just
as costly as thoughtless action. The goal
is not endless analysis. It is useful
analysis followed by decisive movement.
Assess, act, assess again.

FIELD CARD: ASSESSMENT

- What can hurt me the quickest.
- What is changing fastest.
- What information is missing.
- What action buys time.
- What would panic make me do wrong.

FIELD EXERCISE: FASTEST HARM

In one stressful moment, ask: what can
hurt me the quickest. Answer that before
worrying about embarrassment,
inconvenience, or secondary problems.

THE ROGUE:

Most people move through life in a
reactive posture. They go on dates hoping
to be liked, walk into interviews hoping
to impress, and shape themselves around

whatever approval seems available. A
rogue starts from a different premise. He
is not begging the room to validate him.
He is deciding what the room is worth.

That does not mean arrogance for its
own sake. It means self possession. You
stop auditioning. You stop chasing every
sign of approval. You pay attention
instead. Do I like this person. Do I
respect this place. Do I want what is
being offered here at all.

A roguish presence is usually calmer
than people expect. Slower speech, less
fidgeting, fewer explanations, and a
willingness to let silence do some of the
work all signal that you are not
desperate to be accepted. Desperation
invites disrespect. Composure raises your
price.

This is one of the quiet uses of
spycraft in normal life. When you stop
centering the other person's approval and
start centering judgment, perception
shifts. People treat you more seriously
because you are treating yourself that
way first.

FIELD EXERCISE: REFUSE THE AUDITION

In one social situation, stop asking
whether they like you and ask whether you
respect the room, the offer, or the
person. Judgment changes posture.

THE CAMOUFLAGE:

Nothing looks more suspicious than someone trying too hard not to look suspicious. In many environments, the better cover is not stealth but harmless incompetence. People scrutinize prowlers. They wave off the person who seems mildly confused, apologetic, and forgettable.

That is why simple environmental fit beats clever costume work. A delivery uniform, a box, a clipboard, the right shoes, the right pace, and the right level of confidence often do more than any dramatic disguise. Good camouflage is behavior first.

The tone matters. The goal is mild inconvenience, not confrontation. An overdone apology, a small mistake, a request for help, or a harmless misunderstanding can redirect scrutiny because people want the awkward person gone, not examined.

Used correctly, camouflage buys you access and time. The point is not to look brilliant. It is to look ordinary enough that no one bothers to remember you.

FIELD EXERCISE: ORDINARY FIT

Observe one setting and identify what ordinary looks like there: shoes, pace, hands, bag, posture, and attention level. Fit is often behavioral before it is visual.

THE FEELINGS:

Every person you meet is carrying a private world of wants, fears, resentments, hopes, and unfinished business. Most people know that in theory. Very few apply it in practice. Sympathy is common. Real empathy is rarer. Sympathy notices pain. Empathy works to understand it.

That matters because HUMINT is relationship work. Influence starts with understanding what moves someone, not with showing off your own intelligence. If you know what a person is protecting, fearing, craving, or trying to prove, your timing improves and your misreads go down.

MICE remains a useful shorthand for motive. Money is broader than cash and often means relief, convenience, access, or opportunity. Ideology is what a person believes they are serving. Coercion can work, but it is unstable and expensive. Ego is how a person needs to see themselves and how they need others to see them.

FALL adds another layer. Fear, anger, love, and laziness explain far more behavior than people like to admit. A person may act from panic, resentment, devotion, or simple desire for the path of least resistance. Often the cleaner explanation is the right one.

The practical habit is to ask better
questions. What pressure is this person
under. What do they want to preserve.
What loss are they trying to avoid. What
role do they need to inhabit in their own
story. Once you start asking those
questions, behavior becomes easier to
read.

Empathy is still a discipline, not
magic. You do not get there by projecting
your own feelings onto someone else. You
get there by quieting your internal noise
long enough to see the other person
clearly. In tradecraft and in ordinary
life, that kind of understanding is a
force multiplier.

FIELD EXERCISE: PRESSURE QUESTION

When someone behaves strangely, ask what
pressure could be producing it. Fear,
anger, love, laziness, ego, relief, or
avoidance often explains more than
personality labels.

BUG OUT:

Every wave of public panic produces the
same instinct. Get out, get moving, get
supplies. Sometimes that is the right
move. Often it is not. A hurried
evacuation into uncertainty can be more
dangerous than staying put with
preparation, shelter, and home ground
advantage.

Your home holds resources you cannot carry away all at once. It gives you walls, clothing, water, a bathroom, familiar routes, and at least some control over the environment. That matters more than people admit when they romanticize leaving.

The exception is straightforward. If staying places you or your family in credible life threatening danger, leave early and leave with a real destination. Do not confuse realism with bravado. There is no honor in waiting too long and forcing someone else to rescue you.

The practical rule is to prepare for both options while treating panic as the enemy. Build the capacity to shelter in place. Build the capacity to move. Then decide from the facts in front of you instead of the emotional contagion around you.

FIELD EXERCISE: STAY OR GO AUDIT

Write two lists for your home: what helps you stay and what helps you leave. Preparation means both choices are available before emotion chooses for you.

ORDER:

Anarchists and other decentralized actors have often been effective at espionage, sabotage, and disruption because loose systems are harder to map and harder to decapitate. A rigid hierarchy gives an adversary visible points of failure. A diffuse network forces them to work much harder.

The useful concept here is spontaneous order. People with similar pressures, fears, incentives, and opportunities often move in the same direction without a single mastermind coordinating them. That can make small groups look larger, smarter, and more synchronized than they really are.

This matters because panic loves stories of perfect coordination. In reality, many events that look like a grand design are simply many people responding to the same incentives at once. If you misread that, you exaggerate the enemy and misunderstand the terrain.

The practical lesson is to watch mood, incentives, and common pressure points. Once you understand what a population is feeling and where those feelings are likely to channel, behavior becomes easier to predict.

FIELD EXERCISE: INCENTIVE WEATHER

Look at one group behavior and ask what shared pressure could make people move in the same direction without a mastermind. Watch incentives before inventing villains.

COMPETITION:

The moment you start competing with someone, you grant them status. You place them in your lane and treat them as a real peer threat. That can be useful in a fight. In many ordinary settings, it is a needless gift.

A better move is often to refuse the frame. Stay calm, stay useful, and stop organizing your behavior around the idea that this person deserves so much of your attention. Save your real energy for your own standard. People become less intimidating the moment you stop feeding them importance.

FIELD EXERCISE: DENY THE FRAME

When someone tries to pull you into petty competition, do not counterpunch. Stay useful, continue your own standard, and give less attention than the provocation wants.

TECH:

Privacy is not dead, but it is expensive, fragile, and under constant pressure. Convenience keeps winning because most people do not notice the trade until long after they have made it. That is why low tech habits still matter. They reduce exposure without asking you to win a

digital arms race you were never equipped
to fight.

The human element remains the softest
point in most systems. A person can spend
money on encrypted apps and still hand
away access through carelessness, habit,
or social engineering. That is why the
fix is not just software. It is
discipline.

Think in layers. Use better tools where
you can, but do not confuse tools with
invisibility. The less data you generate,
the less data there is to collect, buy,
leak, or steal.

Old school habits still carry weight.
An analog watch, fewer connected devices,
less reflexive posting, less convenience
purchased with constant exposure.
Tradecraft begins when you notice what
you are giving away without meaning to.

P.J. FIELD NOTE

Tools help, but discipline matters more.
A person can buy privacy software and
still give the whole game away through
habit, convenience, and attention hunger.

FIELD EXERCISE: EXPOSURE CUT

Remove one unnecessary data leak today:
an app permission, a public post, an old
account, a saved card, or a location
habit. Less generated data means less
exposed data.

The Question:

Ask why. Ask who benefits. Ask what incentive is hiding beneath the explanation. That habit alone will save you from a great deal of manipulation. The Latin phrase cui bono captures the idea neatly. To whose benefit.

Information does not become worthless because someone has motives. Motives are simply part of the terrain. The mistake is treating information as clean when the incentives around it are dirty. In war, politics, business, and everyday gossip, people often tell the truth for crooked reasons or tell crooked stories for practical gain.

The tradecraft habit is not cynicism for its own sake. It is disciplined curiosity. Ask what this story allows someone to gain, avoid, or redirect. Once you do that consistently, you become much harder to use.

FIELD EXERCISE: CUI BONO

Take one claim, rumor, sales pitch, or political message and ask who benefits if you believe it. Motive is not proof, but it is terrain.

The Prep:

Most procrastination is survivable. Dirty dishes, unmowed grass, and postponed errands usually cost you nothing worse than inconvenience. Safety is different. The things you put off in that category have a way of becoming urgent at the worst possible moment.

A half empty gas tank, neglected maintenance, dead flashlight batteries, expired medical supplies, or rusty self defense habits all feel minor until the day they do not. The danger is rarely the object itself. The danger is the timing. Fatigue, weather, bad neighborhoods, family stress, and pressure stack quickly.

Preparation matters because emergencies do not arrive on a schedule that flatters you. They arrive when you are tired, distracted, cold, rushed, or emotionally overloaded.

So take care of the unglamorous things. Fuel the car. Check the batteries. Maintain the tools. Keep the body and the mind ready. Prepare enough that you can forget about it for a while, because when you need it, it is already there.

FIELD EXERCISE: BORING READINESS

Choose one neglected readiness item and fix it: fuel, flashlight, batteries, documents, first aid, spare key, phone charger, or vehicle maintenance.

ENTRY:

Entryism is the slow capture of an organization from the inside. It is usually discussed in politics, but the method works anywhere people can place loyalists, shift culture, and influence decisions without making a loud bid for power.

That is why it matters beyond politics. A company, nonprofit, club, school, church, or local network can all be reshaped from within if the right people gain position, hire their own, reward their own, and quietly alter the incentives around everyone else.

The practical value is twofold. You can recognize it when it is happening around you, and you can understand why internal placement often changes outcomes more effectively than external pressure.

FIELD EXERCISE: PLACEMENT WATCH

Notice who has informal influence inside one organization. Who hires, rewards, schedules, frames issues, or controls access. Power often enters through ordinary placement.

THE PAINS:

Pain teaches fast. Fear of pain teaches even faster. Human beings avoid physical harm instinctively, but we also bend our

lives around the anticipation of
embarrassment, rejection, humiliation,
and loss. That anticipation can control
us just as effectively as the real thing.

The result is familiar. People tolerate
bad treatment because confrontation feels
painful. They avoid opportunities because
rejection feels painful. They organize
their lives around preventing discomfort
and then wonder why their world keeps
getting smaller.

The answer is controlled exposure.
Physical training teaches this clearly.
Once you have been hit, thrown, choked,
and stressed in training, the unknown
shrinks. The same logic applies to
emotional discomfort. Rejection becomes
less powerful once you have survived
enough of it on purpose.

This is one reason resilient people are
hard to coerce. They have already made
peace with a certain amount of pain. If
you can tolerate discomfort without
panicking, other people lose one of their
easiest handles on you.

FIELD EXERCISE: DISCOMFORT REP

Choose one small discomfort on purpose:
make the call, ask the question, train
hard, accept a no, or have the awkward
conversation. Controlled discomfort
lowers future leverage against you.

GLOMAR:

The Glomar response is one of the most famous evasions in espionage history. Its power comes from controlled ambiguity. It does not fully deny, it does not fully admit, and it leaves the other person with nothing solid to attack.

That is useful because people do not always need a detailed answer. Often they only need enough to feel like the conversation has reached its limit. A calm refusal, a no comment, or a carefully bounded answer can protect privacy without forcing you into a direct lie.

The technique also works because imagination is rarely modest. Once you refuse to resolve a question fully, other people start filling the space themselves. Their projection often creates a bigger story than the truth would have done.

Used well, Glomar style ambiguity can preserve confidentiality, avoid needless conflict, and add a little mystery without surrendering control of the conversation.

FIELD CARD: GLOMAR

- What do I not need to answer.
- What can I acknowledge safely.
- Where is the boundary.

- Can I refuse calmly enough that the conversation feels finished.

FIELD EXERCISE: BOUNDED ANSWER

Practice one calm refusal: I am not going to get into that. Keep your tone ordinary and do not fill the silence with excuses.

SUCCESSES:

Intelligence services benefit from asymmetry in reputation. Their failures become public. Their successes often stay hidden. That sounds unfair until you notice what secrecy also buys them. Legend. Ambiguity. The ability to be overestimated by some people and underestimated by others.

That same dynamic appears in ordinary life. Quiet competence often creates a larger myth than loud self promotion. People fill in the blanks. They assume the reserved person knows more, has done more, or can do more than the person who keeps explaining themselves.

The practical lesson is not to fabricate grandiosity. It is to let solid work travel through other people when it can. Downplay a little. Avoid overexplaining. Let reputation build from residue.

Mystique is not the goal in itself. But when people cannot easily map your ceiling, they tend to treat you with more care. In many situations, that is useful.

FIELD EXERCISE: QUIET PROOF

Do one useful thing well and resist explaining it. Let the result travel farther than the announcement.

THE RULES:

Espionage services accumulate rules the way fighting cultures accumulate scar tissue. Some are time bound. Some are timeless. The enduring ones usually point back to the same fundamentals.

First, remain undetected when you can. A dead operative is useless. A captured one can be worse. Tradecraft begins with not forcing the dramatic option in the first place.

Behave casually. People notice strain, urgency, and curiosity faster than they notice competence. The more natural you look inside the role, the less attention the role attracts.

Show little interest. Overeagerness is memorable. Quiet attention is harder to read and easier to sustain. You can learn a great deal while appearing only mildly engaged.

Play the part with consistency. A cover does not fail because the broad outline is wrong. It fails because the small habits do not match. The same principle applies in ordinary life. Inconsistency draws eyes.

Keep your wits hidden under the surface. Be the wise man playing the fool, not the fool who got carried away by his own act. Deception should not deceive you.

Revise fast. Plans matter, but conditions change. Do not worship the route so much that you miss what the terrain is telling you.

Protect identity, freedom, and mobility. If a choice satisfies your ego but burns those three, it is probably a bad trade.

The throughline is simple. Good tradecraft is usually quiet, flexible, and harder to notice than people expect.

FIELD EXERCISE: RULE OF THREE

Choose three rules from this section and apply them for one day: behave casually, show little interest, revise fast, protect mobility, or keep your wits under the surface.

THE ENGAGEMENT:

Danger does not produce one neat response. Fight or flight is too simple. Human beings freeze, posture, appease, misread, overreact, and sometimes do nothing at all. That is normal. The question is not whether stress hits you. The question is how quickly you can regain useful behavior once it does.

Training matters because the unfamiliar overwhelms. The more violence, chaos, or pressure feels alien, the more likely you are to lock up or burn energy on the wrong response. Familiarity shrinks shock.

That is why exposure training matters in self defense, emergency work, and high pressure decision making. You do not need to become fearless. You need to become functional faster.

The practical rule is to expect your first surge of stress and then work through it. Breathe, orient, move, and get back to useful choices before panic makes the choices for you.

FIELD EXERCISE: FUNCTION FASTER

When stress rises, name the next useful action out loud or in your head: breathe, move, call, leave, lock, ask, or cover. The first useful verb breaks the freeze.

THE DECEPTION:

Deception has tactical uses, but it also has a cost. Every lie makes the next lie easier and makes your foundation a little weaker. Even when a deception works, it can still train you in the wrong direction.

That is why truthfulness remains practical, not just moral. A person known for honesty can use omission, silence, or narrow disclosure when needed and still retain credibility. A person known for casual deception loses that reserve.

If you want to detect deceit in others, do not chase movie tells. Baseline matters more than folklore. People leak stress in different ways. The useful question is whether behavior changed, not whether it matches a cliché.

FIELD CARD: THE DECEPTION

- What is normal for this person.
- What changed.
- What question creates pressure without accusation.
- What would I need to verify before I decide.

FIELD EXERCISE: BASELINE CHECK

Before deciding someone is lying, identify their normal. Then identify the deviation. Suspicion without baseline becomes superstition.

THE HANGOUT:

I try to avoid lying. Omission is different. Silence, selective disclosure, and a well framed answer can protect privacy without forcing you into outright falsehood. That distinction matters more than people think.

In practical life, this often means answering the useful part of a question while withholding what does not belong to

the person asking. Reassure safety, state
the limit, and stop there. Most people
only push further when your first answer
creates more drama than clarity.

That is why the limited hangout works.
You disclose enough to settle the moment
while keeping the deeper detail where it
belongs. It is less glamorous than spy
fiction makes it sound, but it is one of
the cleanest ways to protect privacy and
confidentiality.

The rule is simple. Give away what
serves the situation. Keep what does not.
Do it calmly enough that the boundary
feels ordinary.

FIELD EXERCISE: USEFUL DISCLOSURE

Answer one intrusive question by giving
only what serves the situation. Do not
lie. Do not overpay with detail.

CIVILIAN OPERATION: QUIET NO

Someone asks a question that reaches past
their need to know. The social pressure
is immediate. You want to answer because
silence feels rude, and you want to
overexplain because overexplaining feels
like safety. That is the trap.

Give a useful answer and stop. If they
ask why you are not available, you can
say, "I have a commitment I need to
keep." If they ask about a private family
matter, you can say, "It is being
handled, but I appreciate you asking."

Calm limits work best when they do not invite debate.

The operational principle is simple. You can be polite without surrendering the file. Privacy does not require hostility. It requires a sentence that closes the door without slamming it.

TIMING:

Most people think advantage belongs to the strongest move. More often it belongs to the right move at the right moment. Too early looks aggressive. Too late looks weak. Tradecraft lives in the interval between those two errors.

Timing depends on patience, observation, and restraint. Speak after you understand the room. Ask after the other person has signaled what they care about. Leave before the environment turns against you. Push only when the other side has already started leaning your way. In ordinary life, good timing makes modest tools look powerful.

That is also why self control matters so much throughout this library. You cannot time anything well while you are desperate to be heard, eager to impress, or too emotional to wait. Calm buys you a fraction of a second. A fraction of a second buys better judgment. Better judgment is often the whole game.

P.J. FIELD NOTE

Timing is the least dramatic advantage and often the decisive one. A calmer person wins small intervals all day. Those intervals become leverage.

FIELD CARD: TIMING

• Is the room ready.
• Has the other person shown what they care about.
• Will speaking now improve position or merely discharge emotion.
• What happens if I wait ten seconds.

FIELD EXERCISE: TEN SECOND ADVANTAGE

Before sending a reactive text, email, or answer, wait ten seconds and revise for position. You are not trying to be slower. You are buying judgment.

THE P.J. AGNESS TRADECRAFT LEXICON

This lexicon keeps the language practical. Use the terms as handles for behavior, not as costume pieces.

Access: The ability to reach a person, place, system, conversation, or opportunity. Trust often creates access before authority does.

Baseline: The normal pattern for a person, place, group, or routine.

Deviation matters only after normal has been learned.

Cover: A lawful privacy frame that explains your presence or protects unnecessary detail. Good cover stays close to truth and remains boring.

Cutout: A separation point that keeps one person, system, or detail from exposing another. In ordinary life, it can be as simple as separating public information from private family information.

Field Card: A short operational checklist used before, during, or after pressure. It turns a concept into action.

Glomar: A controlled refusal to confirm or deny. Useful when answering either way would surrender too much.

Limited Hangout: A partial, truthful disclosure that settles the moment without opening the entire file.

MICE: Money, ideology, coercion, and ego. A motive framework for understanding what may move a person.

Position: Your physical, social, informational, and psychological standing. Improve position before forcing outcomes.

Signal: Information that changes risk, timing, motive, or position. Everything else is noise until proven otherwise.

Tradecraft: The disciplined use of awareness, information, timing, behavior, and position to preserve options and act cleanly.

Trust Bank: The accumulated credit
created by reliability, discretion,
usefulness, and kept promises.

SPECIAL EDITION FIELD DRILLS

Use these drills as short repetitions, not performances. A drill is successful when the behavior becomes quieter, faster, and more natural.

The Baseline Drill: Spend five minutes observing a familiar place before judging anything unusual. Learn normal first.

The Exit Count Drill: Count exits in every room you enter for one day. Do it without turning your head like a lighthouse.

The Name Recall Drill: Learn three names and use each one naturally before the interaction ends.

The Three-Question Motive Drill: Ask what the person wants, fears, and needs to protect.

The Route Variation Drill: Change one regular route or timing pattern without making your life harder.

The Quiet Confidence Drill: Speak slightly slower, answer once, and stop adding proof after the point is made.

The No-Overexplaining Drill: Give one clean answer and let it stand. Do not chase approval with extra detail.

The Crowded Room Position Drill: Stand where you can see the entrance and leave without fighting the flow.

The Public Place SDR Drill: Use harmless route changes in a public space to notice repeated movement. Do not confront. Do not escalate.

The Information Audit Drill: Separate known facts from assumptions before making a decision.

The Glomar Drill: Practice a calm boundary answer to a question that deserves no full answer.

The Timing Drill: Delay one reactive message long enough to improve the frame.

The Trust Deposit Drill: Keep one small promise quickly.

The Cover Story Drill: Create a one-degree privacy answer that stays close to truth and remains boring.

The Propaganda Weather Drill: Identify the emotion a message wants before judging its argument.

The Object Use Drill: Identify three ordinary objects that could buy distance or time in an emergency.

The Friction Drill: Remove one small piece of needless complexity from a routine.

The Pressure Drill: Ask what pressure explains a behavior before assuming character explains it.

The Exposure Drill: Reduce one digital, social, or routine exposure today.

The Exit Early Drill: Leave one situation before your options get worse.

THE 30-DAY SPYCRAFT CHALLENGE

This challenge turns the book into a month of field practice. Keep it lawful, ordinary, and quiet. The point is not to become theatrical. The point is to become more observant and harder to rush.

Day 1: Count exits in every public room.

Day 2: Learn and use three names.

Day 3: Identify one baseline in a person or place you know well.

Day 4: Change one predictable route or timing pattern.

Day 5: Answer one intrusive question with a calm limited answer.

Day 6: Map one problem through trust, access, information, timing, position, options, and control.

Day 7: Make one small reliability deposit with another person.

Day 8: Observe a crowd from the edge and identify the flow.

Day 9: Remove one unnecessary app permission or digital exposure.

Day 10: Practice the ten-second pause before a reactive response.

Day 11: Identify the person who controls access in a room, workplace, or system.

Day 12: Run the four-question information audit on a stressful message.

Day 13: Notice one persuasive message and name the emotion it wants.

Day 14: Create one one-degree privacy answer for a question you dislike.

Day 15: Identify cover and concealment in one ordinary place.

Day 16: Ask two open questions in a conversation and listen for motive.

Day 17: Reduce one overcomplicated plan to three next actions.

Day 18: Fix one boring readiness item you have neglected.

Day 19: Make one useful local contact warmer than it was yesterday.

Day 20: Practice leaving a situation before it becomes annoying, crowded, or unstable.

Day 21: Identify one source of needless friction and remove it.

Day 22: Watch one organization and identify informal influence.

Day 23: Do one useful thing well without announcing it.

Day 24: Practice calm refusal without filling the silence.

Day 25: Identify one discomfort you avoid and take a small controlled rep against it.

Day 26: Observe ordinary camouflage in a setting: shoes, pace, posture, bag, and attention.

Day 27: Sort one room into defensive tools, distraction tools, and distance tools.

Day 28: Find one situation where competition is a trap and refuse the frame.

Day 29: Review your notes and identify the skill that changed your behavior most.

Day 30: Build your personal spycraft rule set: five habits you will keep.

THE FINAL FIELD EXAM

This is not a certification. It is a reality check. If the book has done its job, these skills should feel less like concepts and more like ordinary behavior.

1. Enter a room and identify the main entrance, nearest usable exit, and likely bottleneck without staring.

2. Learn three names in ordinary interactions and use them naturally once.

3. Watch a familiar person or place long enough to identify baseline before judging deviation.

4. Receive a stressful message and separate facts, claims, assumptions, and emotional weather before answering.

5. Improve position in a conversation without raising volume, issuing threats, or chasing approval.

6. Decline one intrusive question with a truthful limited answer and no extra performance.

7. Spot one pattern in your routine that makes you easier to study, then change it without making life harder.

8. Identify what moves a person in a low-stakes interaction: convenience, ego, fear, duty, affection, money, or pressure.

9. Leave one situation early because the mood, crowd, timing, or exits are getting worse.

10. Explain the operating chain from memory: trust, access, information, timing, position, options, control.

Passing the exam does not mean you become theatrical. It means your ordinary behavior has become harder to exploit and easier to trust.

THE EVERYDAY SPYCRAFT DOSSIER

Use this dossier as a periodic self-audit. The questions are not meant to make life paranoid. They are meant to help you notice where your options are strong and where your habits are leaking advantage.

THE TRUST MAP

• Who trusts you with access, information, or responsibility.

• Where have you earned that trust through proof rather than talk.

• Where is trust being spent faster than it is being replenished.

• What small act would strengthen the relationship without looking strategic.

THE INFORMATION MAP

• What information improves your next decision.

• What information is merely interesting.

• What assumption keeps returning without proof.

• What source has earned confidence and what source has only earned attention.

THE POSITION MAP

• Where are you physically, socially, informationally, and psychologically exposed.

• Who can block your movement, distort your information, or force your timing.

• What move improves options without creating unnecessary conflict.

The Influence Map

• Who shapes the room before decisions are made.
• What emotion moves the group most often.
• Which incentives are visible and which ones are quiet.
• Where would a small frame change produce a large result.

The Personal Security Map

• What patterns make you easy to study.
• What places leave you with poor exits.
• What habits expose your schedule, location, money, or relationships.
• What simple change reduces risk without making life smaller.

The Privacy Map

• What questions do you answer too fully.
• What details do you give away for convenience or approval.
• What information belongs only to you, your family, or a trusted circle.
• What calm sentence protects that boundary.

The Control Map

• What reliably makes you reactive.
• Where do you talk too much, move too fast, or accept a bad frame.
• What pause, phrase, or routine returns you to useful behavior.

Special Edition Case Files

The following case files are not stories about secret operations. They are civilian pressure tests. Each one takes a principle from this manual and places it inside an ordinary moment where most people either drift, overreact, or give away position without noticing. Read them slowly. The point is not to memorize the scene. The point is to recognize the pattern when a similar one appears in your own life.

Every case file follows the same working sequence: situation, field read, move, and debrief. That order matters. If you skip the field read, you act from impulse. If you skip the move, you become an observer with no effect on the terrain. If you skip the debrief, you repeat mistakes and call them personality.

Case File 1: The Coffee Counter

Situation: You enter a busy coffee shop during a morning rush. The line is long, the staff is moving quickly, and the mood of the room is impatient but not hostile. Most customers treat the workers like machinery. They stare at phones, bark orders, and act annoyed that other human beings are involved in the process.

Field read: The staff is under time
pressure. The customer in front of you is
irritated. The employee at the register
has already absorbed too much small
disrespect before you arrived. Nothing
dangerous is happening, but the social
temperature is low. This is a clean place
to practice trust, names, and small
humanization without performing for
anyone.

Move: When it is your turn, slow down
slightly. Use a normal tone. If the
employee has a name tag, use the name
once. If the order is simple, keep it
simple. If there is a small error,
correct it without making the employee
pay an emotional tax. You are not trying
to charm the room. You are trying to
become the easiest person in the line to
deal with.

Debrief: This is low-risk HUMINT in
ordinary clothes. The lesson is not that
every barista becomes an asset. The
lesson is that trust deposits begin in
small interactions. People remember the
person who lowers friction. In a
different setting, that same habit opens
doors, softens resistance, and makes
later requests easier because your first
signal was steadiness.

CASE FILE 2: THE EXIT SEAT

Situation: You meet someone at a
restaurant. The room is pleasant, the
conversation matters, and there is no
obvious threat. Most people choose the

first comfortable seat and then surrender the environment for the rest of the meal. They face a wall, ignore the entrance, and let the room become scenery.

Field read: The entrance is to your right. A hallway leads to restrooms and a side exit. The server station sits between you and the kitchen. Two tables are loud, one corner is quiet, and the bar has the highest emotional movement in the room. None of this requires staring. It requires one clean scan when you enter, then normal behavior.

Move: Choose a seat that lets you see the entrance without making it theatrical. Notice the exits once and then stop advertising awareness. Keep your phone away unless you need it. Listen to the person you came to meet. If the mood of the room changes, you already know your options because you paid attention before urgency arrived.

Debrief: Environmental mastery is not paranoia. It is respect for future choices. The person who waits until trouble starts to find the exits has already wasted time. The person who notices early can stay relaxed because the important questions are answered before the room gets loud.

CASE FILE 3: THE BAD MEETING

Situation: You are pulled into a meeting where someone wants momentum more than clarity. The language sounds confident, but the proposal is vague.

Several people are nodding because nobody wants to be the one who slows the room. This is how bad plans recruit good people.

Field read: The pressure is social, not factual. The room wants agreement. The decision maker has attached ego to speed. The risk is not only the plan itself. The risk is being recorded mentally as either cooperative or difficult before the facts have been sorted.

Move: Do not attack the proposal. Ask a clean question that protects everyone. Try, "What would have to be true for this to work?" or "What is the first failure point we should plan around?" Those questions make caution useful instead of oppositional. You are not refusing the frame. You are forcing the frame to carry weight.

Debrief: Position in a meeting is often informational. The person who asks the better question can slow a weak plan without becoming the villain. This is tradecraft in administrative clothing: reduce emotion, isolate the real issue, and move the room from performance to evidence.

CASE FILE 4: THE INTRUSIVE QUESTION

Situation: Someone asks a question that reaches past their right to know. It may happen at work, in a family conversation, during a date, or inside a casual social exchange. The question arrives with a friendly tone, which makes refusal feel rude.

Field read: The danger is not the question alone. The danger is your reflex to answer fully because silence feels awkward. Many people surrender private information not because they chose to share it, but because they could not tolerate two seconds of discomfort.

Move: Answer the useful part and stop. "I have it handled." "That is still being sorted out." "I am not getting into the details, but the situation is under control." Keep your voice ordinary. Do not apologize for the boundary. Do not overexplain the boundary. Overexplaining often reopens the door you just closed.

Debrief: Privacy is a discipline. The limited hangout works because it gives the other person enough to settle the moment without handing them the deeper file. You do not owe every curious person a full report on your life.

CASE FILE 5: THE PARKING LOT

Situation: You leave a store at night. The lot is mostly open, with a few idling cars and scattered shoppers. You are tired, carrying bags, and thinking about the next errand. This is exactly when people stop seeing the ground they are standing on.

Field read: The light is uneven. Your hands are occupied. A vehicle is idling near the row you need to cross. A person near the cart return appears to be waiting, but not necessarily for you. None of this proves danger. It does mean you should improve position before you commit to a path.

Move: Free one hand before leaving the doorway. Put keys where you can reach them without digging. Walk with purpose, not speed. If a route feels off, change it early, while options are still easy. If needed, wait near the entrance, ask an employee for help, or move with other people rather than isolating yourself between cars.

Debrief: Safety is often decided before contact. A better route, a free hand, and one extra minute of patience can prevent the moment that later requires force. The goal is not bravery in the lot. The goal is not needing bravery because you kept your options open.

CASE FILE 6: THE MESSAGE LEAK

Situation: You have a small circle of people who receive sensitive information before everyone else. A personal plan leaks. You do not know who passed it along. Anger tells you to confront everyone. Tradecraft tells you to map the channel.

Field read: The leak may not be malicious. It may be careless. People repeat information to gain status, bond with others, or relieve their own excitement. The motive matters later. First you need to identify the route.

Move: Use a canary trap only with lawful, harmless information. Give slightly different versions of a minor detail to different people. Do not fabricate anything that harms others or creates real consequences. Then wait. If one version returns through another channel, you have learned something about distribution without launching a dramatic accusation.

Debrief: Information control is not suspicion for its own sake. It is stewardship. When a fact matters, control where it goes and learn how it travels. Loose lips are not always hostile, but they are still operationally expensive.

CASE FILE 7: THE CROWD SHIFT

Situation: You are at an outdoor event. The crowd is relaxed at first. Then a noise, argument, announcement, or rumor changes the mood. People begin looking in the same direction. Phones go up. Movement slows near one area and speeds up near another.

Field read: The crowd is becoming a single nervous organism. You do not need to know the full story yet. You need to avoid the center of movement. The first useful question is not "What happened?" It is "Where is the edge?"

Move: Angle calmly toward the perimeter before everyone decides to move at once. Do not push into the flow to satisfy curiosity. Do not stand still in a channel where movement is forming behind you. If you are with others, give simple directions: "We are moving this way now."

Debrief: Crowds punish hesitation. The person who waits for perfect information often loses physical position. Early, calm movement toward the edge is not panic. It is timing.

CASE FILE 8: THE FAVOR

Situation: You need help from someone who has no formal obligation to give it. Most people make this clumsy. They either beg, flatter, or explain their own problem so intensely that the other person feels trapped.

Field read: The other person is protecting time, status, energy, or reputation. Your need is not their motive. If you want cooperation, you need to make the request easy to understand, easy to refuse, and connected to a benefit or clean purpose they can accept.

Move: Lead with their frame. "This may save you a headache later." "This should keep the process cleaner for both of us." "A quick look from you would help me avoid creating extra work." Then ask for one specific action. Small, clean requests get better results than vague emotional pressure.

Debrief: Influence improves when ego gets out of the way. The best ask is not a speech about your need. It is a clear doorway the other person can walk through without feeling used.

CASE FILE 9: THE DIGITAL CONVENIENCE TRAP

Situation: An app, website, or device offers convenience in exchange for more access than the task requires. Most people accept because the friction is small and the benefit is immediate. The cost is delayed, distributed, and easy to ignore.

Field read: The question is not whether the tool is evil. The question is whether the exposure is proportional. Contacts, location, photos, microphone access, and account linking should never become automatic yeses just because the button is easy.

Move: Pause before granting access. Use the narrowest setting that still lets the tool function. Turn off permissions you do not need. Separate accounts when possible. Reduce the amount of data your routine produces. Do not confuse convenience with innocence.

Debrief: Privacy is rarely lost in one dramatic breach. It is surrendered through a thousand convenient taps. The less you generate, the less there is to collect, buy, leak, or use against you.

CASE FILE 10: THE FALSE COMPETITION

Situation: Someone treats you like a rival and tries to pull you into a contest you did not choose. It may be social, professional, romantic, or political. Their goal may be victory, but often it is recognition. They want the status that comes from being taken seriously as an equal threat.

Field read: The contest itself may be the trap. If you engage too quickly, you grant status and attention. If you ignore the person carelessly, you may miss a real move. The right read separates noise from consequence.

Move: Do not mirror their urgency. Track actions, not tone. Respond only to material behavior. Keep doing the work. If a boundary must be set, set it cleanly and without theatrical heat. The refusal to compete is not weakness when your position is stronger outside the frame.

Debrief: Not every challenge deserves your sword. Some people are fed by your reaction. Denying the frame preserves energy and keeps your standard from being dragged into someone else's performance.

CASE FILE 11: THE QUIET NO

Situation: You need to refuse a request without creating unnecessary hostility. The request is not evil, but it is too expensive, too invasive, or too poorly timed. Many people either surrender or refuse with too much force.

Field read: The other person may be testing how much pressure works on you. They may also simply be asking because asking costs them nothing. Your job is to answer without leaking guilt, anger, or excess detail.

Move: Use a calm, narrow sentence. "I cannot do that." "That does not work for me." "I am going to pass." If the situation requires a small explanation, give one, then stop. Do not build a courtroom defense. A clean no loses power when you bury it under nervous exhibits.

Debrief: Boundaries become easier to respect when they sound ordinary. The goal is not dominance. The goal is freedom of action without unnecessary debris.

CASE FILE 12: THE AFTER-ACTION REVIEW

Situation: A difficult conversation or minor conflict ends. Most people immediately begin defending themselves internally. They replay the other person's worst line, justify their own reaction, and call the process reflection.

Field read: Emotional replay is not analysis. It preserves heat. A real debrief reduces the event to usable information. What happened. What did you miss. What did you handle well. What would improve the next encounter.

Move: Write three lines. First, the fact pattern without adjectives. Second, the moment where your position improved or collapsed. Third, the next behavioral adjustment. Keep it short enough that you will actually do it.

Debrief: A person who debriefs cleanly becomes difficult to keep fooling. Every encounter becomes training. Every awkward moment becomes signal. That is how small mistakes become expensive only once.

THE SPECIAL EDITION FIELD WORKBOOK

This workbook section turns the manual into paper you can actually use. Do not make it precious. Mark it up. Circle weak points. Write ugly notes. The value is not in keeping the page clean. The value is in forcing your attention onto the parts of life that normally remain vague until they become problems.

Use these pages after reading the manual, during the 30-day challenge, or after any situation that leaves a residue in your head. A good field note is brief, factual, and pointed toward the next move.

WORKBOOK PAGE 1: PERSONAL BASELINE

Use this page to establish your own normal before you try to improve it. People often build plans around an imaginary version of themselves. Start with the real one.

What situations make me reactive?
Where do I overexplain?
Where do I trust too quickly?

What places or routines make me easy to
predict?
What one habit would improve my position
fastest?
    Field note:

____

____

    Adjustment:

____

____

    Date reviewed:

____

______

WORKBOOK PAGE 2: THE ROOM SCAN

    Use this page after entering any public
place you visit often. The goal is to
train quiet environmental literacy, not
to turn yourself into a person who stares
at doors all night.

Main entrance:

____

___

Secondary exits:

____

Likely bottlenecks:

____

Best calm seat or position:

____

Worst trapped position:

____

What would change if the mood shifted?

____

One improvement next time:

____

WORKBOOK PAGE 3: THE TRUST LEDGER

Trust is not a mood. It is a ledger
built from repeated evidence. Use this
page to map where you are making
deposits, where you are creating doubt,
and where you are asking for more trust
than you have earned.

Person or group:

____

What do they need from me to feel safe or
confident? _________
What have I done that proves reliability?

____

What have I done that weakens confidence?

____

One small deposit I can make this week:

____

One overpromise I should stop making:

____

Debrief:

____

____

WORKBOOK PAGE 4: THE INFORMATION AUDIT

Information becomes useful only after it is ranked. Use this page when a situation feels noisy, urgent, emotional, or politically loaded.

What do I know?

____

—

What do I only think I know?

____

What is the source?

____

What matters right now?

____

What can wait?

____

——

What would change my next move?

____

   Decision:

____

____

WORKBOOK PAGE 5: THE PRIVACY BOUNDARY

Use this page to prepare before you need it. A privacy boundary built under pressure usually leaks. A sentence prepared ahead of time is easier to deliver calmly.

Topic I do not need to discuss fully:

____

Who tends to ask about it?

____

What useful part can I answer safely?

____

What detail should remain private?

____

My calm boundary sentence:

____

My repeat sentence if pushed:

____

  Practice date:

____

____

WORKBOOK PAGE 6: THE POSITION IMPROVEMENT PLAN

Use this when a problem feels larger than your current options. Do not begin by asking how to win. Begin by asking how to improve position.

Current problem:

____

Where am I exposed?

____

Who controls access?

____

Who controls information?

____

What small move gives me more options?

____

What emotional move would make this worse?

____

   First action:

____

____

WORKBOOK PAGE 7: THE AFTER-ACTION REVIEW

   Use this after a conflict, awkward
interaction, safety concern, or important
decision. Keep it factual. The goal is
learning, not self-punishment.

What happened, without drama?

____

What did I notice early?

____

What did I miss?

____

Where did I improve position?

____

Where did I leak position?

____

What will I do differently next time?

____

   Doctrine line from this event:

____

WORKBOOK PAGE 8: THE WEEKLY FIELD REVIEW

Use this once a week while working through the book. The goal is not to master everything at once. The goal is to carry one better habit into the next week.

Best read of the week:

____

Worst misread of the week:

____

One privacy win:

____

One trust deposit:

____

One position improvement:

____

One habit to practice next week:

____

Review date:

____

____

ADDITIONAL FIELD NOTES FOR THE PAPERBACK EDITION

The paperback version gives the manual a different function than the ebook. A digital book can be searched. A physical manual can be handled, marked, returned to, and used as a small training object. That matters for material like this

because the goal is not merely
remembering ideas. The goal is building
habits that survive distraction.

Do not try to practice every skill at
once. Pick one category at a time. If you
are poor at environmental awareness, work
exits and position for two weeks. If you
leak too much information, work privacy
and limited answers. If you are socially
sharp but physically careless, work
movement, crowds, and escape. The manual
is a shelf of tools, not a single speech.

The fastest way to waste this material
is to turn it into identity. Do not
become the person who talks about
spycraft constantly. Become the person
who notices faster, speaks cleaner, keeps
better boundaries, and moves a little
earlier than everyone else. The useful
version rarely announces itself.

The second fastest way to waste it is
to chase intensity. Ordinary life
provides enough terrain. Work with coffee
counters, parking lots, meetings, crowded
events, awkward questions, noisy group
chats, bad incentives, and small
decisions under pressure. If a principle
does not survive ordinary life, it is not
ready for anything harder.

A field manual should get dirty. Fold a
corner. Mark a weak sentence. Write a
date next to a drill you actually tried.
Cross out advice that does not fit your
life after honest testing. Add a better
line if you find one. The book becomes

more valuable when it starts carrying evidence that you used it.

The final measure is simple. After thirty days, you should be harder to rush, harder to read, harder to corner, and easier to trust. Not dramatic. Not theatrical. Just better positioned.

INSTRUCTOR BRIEFINGS FOR FIELD USE

The most useful training often happens after the main lesson, when the reader stops asking whether the concept is interesting and starts asking where it belongs in the day. These briefings are meant to close that gap. They are not new categories of spycraft. They are pressure lenses. Each one points back to the same operating chain: trust, access, information, timing, position, options, and control.

Use these briefings when a principle feels too abstract. The test is always practical. What does this change when you walk into a room, answer a question, read a person, protect a private fact, or leave before the environment turns against you?

BRIEFING 1: YOU ARE ALWAYS MANAGING EXPOSURE

Exposure is broader than visibility. You can be physically visible and still protected if your position is good, your information is limited, and your exit remains available. You can also be physically hidden and still exposed if your pattern is obvious, your temper is easy to trigger, or your private information is scattered across people who should never have received it.

Most people think of exposure only when danger feels dramatic. That is too late. Exposure begins in small habits. A predictable route. A public argument. A casual confession to someone who has not earned it. A phone full of unnecessary permissions. A workplace pattern everyone can read. None of these things feels like a crisis when it happens. Together they form a map.

The field habit is simple: ask what you are making available. Your location, mood, priorities, schedule, relationships, fears, and incentives are all information. You do not need to become secretive about everything. You do need to stop treating exposure as neutral. Some information should be public. Some should be earned. Some should never leave your control at all.

Briefing 2: Calm Is Not Passivity

Calm is often misunderstood as softness. It is not. Calm is the condition that lets you act with timing instead of impulse. A person who is calm can refuse, leave, confront, question, or move faster than a reactive person because less energy is being burned on performance.

Passivity waits for permission. Calm buys judgment. The difference matters. You can be calm and still decisive. You can be calm and still dangerous if danger requires it. You can be calm and still say no with no decoration around the word. The point is not to reduce force forever. The point is to keep force attached to choice.

In ordinary life, most bad outcomes are helped along by a loss of emotional command. People answer too much because silence feels tense. They escalate because insult feels unbearable. They stay because leaving feels awkward. They agree because disagreement feels socially expensive. Calm interrupts that chain. It creates the small internal distance where a better option can appear.

BRIEFING 3: CLEVERNESS IS OVERRATED

Clever plans have a vanity problem. They make the planner feel sharp before the plan has touched reality. Simple plans are less flattering, but they survive contact better. This is why good tradecraft often looks boring. The route is simple. The answer is short. The cover story is close to the truth. The exit is chosen before the drama begins.

The clever person wants elegance. The competent person wants reliability. In a real room with real pressure, reliability wins more often. A sentence you can remember under stress is better than a brilliant answer you can only deliver when calm. A plan your family understands is better than a perfect plan no one follows. A boundary you can repeat is better than a speech that depends on mood.

This does not mean dull thinking. It means disciplined design. The skill is reducing the problem until the next action is clean. What matters now. What can wait. What improves position. What protects freedom of action. When those questions are answered, cleverness becomes optional.

BRIEFING 4: PEOPLE LEAK THEIR PRIORITIES

Most people announce what they care about long before they say it directly. They repeat certain complaints. They return to certain fears. They defend certain images of themselves. They hurry around some topics and slow down around others. Those leaks are not always dramatic, but they are useful.

This is why listening beats performance. The person trying to sound interesting usually misses what the other person is revealing. The person who listens for motive begins to hear the machinery under the words. Money, ideology, coercion, ego, fear, anger, love, and laziness are not abstract categories. They are working pressures inside daily behavior.

Do not weaponize this too quickly. First, understand it. A person who needs respect will respond differently than a person who needs relief. A person protecting status will hear a request differently than someone protecting time. When you understand the pressure, your timing improves. When timing improves, influence requires less force.

BRIEFING 5: THE ROOM HAS A MEMORY

Every environment teaches people how to behave inside it. A workplace remembers who gets punished for honesty. A family remembers which topics cause explosions. A bar remembers which regulars are trouble. A neighborhood remembers which house helps and which house watches. The room is not just walls and furniture. It is accumulated behavior.

When you enter a place, read its memory. Where do people hesitate? Who gets deference without speaking loudly? Where does attention go when a certain person enters? What subject makes the air change? These are not mystical signals. They are social tracks worn into the floor by repeated experience.

This matters because many mistakes come from treating every room as neutral. No room is neutral. Each has incentives, taboos, routes, chokepoints, leaders, followers, and ghosts. The person who learns the room before trying to change it wastes less effort.

Briefing 6: Exit Is a Standard, Not a Failure

Leaving is often treated as defeat because ego hates unfinished business. Tradecraft sees it differently. Leaving with options intact is frequently the correct move. The argument can wait. The crowd can keep its mood. The meeting can survive without your last sentence. The street can have the strange person on it after you change direction.

Exit is not always physical. Sometimes it is conversational. Sometimes it is informational. Sometimes it is emotional. You can exit a topic, a frame, a pattern, a power struggle, or a decision cycle that is moving too fast. The skill is recognizing the moment before the price of staying rises.

A useful standard is this: if remaining gives away identity, freedom, mobility, privacy, or judgment for no real gain, leave the frame. You do not need to win every scene. You need to preserve the ability to choose the next one.

Advanced Civilian Operations

These operations are larger than the earlier case files. They place multiple principles together so you can see how the chain works under real social pressure. Read each operation as a small field problem. The correct answer is not always action. Sometimes the correct

answer is waiting, reducing exposure, or
refusing the wrong frame.

OPERATION 1: THE FAMILY INTERROGATION

Situation: A family gathering turns
into a soft interrogation. The questions
sound casual, but the pattern is
familiar. One person keeps pushing for
information about money, relationships,
conflict, health, work, or plans that you
have not chosen to share. Other people
listen because private information is
social entertainment when it belongs to
someone else.

Field read: The setting is emotionally
loaded because family history gives
questions extra leverage. A stranger
asking the same thing might be easy to
refuse. A relative can make refusal feel
like betrayal. The danger is not only
disclosure. It is being pulled into an
old role where you explain, defend,
apologize, or perform adulthood for
people who already have a fixed story
about you.

Move: Refuse the old role before you
answer the question. Keep the tone light
and narrow. "I am keeping that private
for now." "Nothing useful to report
there." "That is not dinner-table
material." Then redirect to a safer topic
or ask the other person something about
themselves. If they push, repeat the
boundary with less language, not more.

Debrief: Familiarity is one of the
strongest pressure tools in ordinary

life. People who knew an earlier version of you often assume continued access to the current version. You can love people and still keep compartments. Privacy does not become rudeness just because the person asking shares your bloodline.

OPERATION 2: THE WORKPLACE WHISPER

Situation: A coworker brings you a rumor. It may be about leadership, another employee, a coming change, or a conflict that has not reached you officially. The information feels useful because it gives you a sense of being inside the stream. It also asks for a response.

Field read: Rumor is both information and bait. It may contain signal, but it also tries to recruit you emotionally. If you react strongly, your reaction becomes information that can travel with the rumor. If you repeat it, you become part of the distribution network. If you dismiss it too quickly, you may miss a real shift in the environment.

Move: Separate receipt from endorsement. Say little. Ask source questions. "Where did that come from?" "Who has actually said this out loud?" "What would change if it were true?" Do not add heat. Do not contribute a more dramatic version. If the rumor concerns something serious, move toward official clarification or documented channels rather than hallway theater.

Debrief: The person who carries rumor without adding to it becomes harder to use. You can collect signal without becoming the loudest instrument in the room. That is information discipline.

OPERATION 3: THE FIRST DATE READ

Situation: You meet someone for a first date or early social interaction. Most people approach the moment as an audition. They try to be liked, funny, attractive, agreeable, and impressive. That internal focus makes them worse at the one job that matters: observation.

Field read: You are not only being evaluated. You are evaluating. How does the person treat staff. Do they ask questions or perform monologues. Do they respect small boundaries. Do they become cruel when inconvenienced. Do they seem curious about the real you or only responsive to the role they want you to play.

Move: Stay warm but not desperate. Ask open questions. Notice whether their answers make room for you. Let silence breathe for a second before rescuing it. Do not overdisclose to create artificial intimacy. If something feels off, do not argue with your own read just because the evening is otherwise pleasant.

Debrief: Attraction can fog judgment because it rewards hope. Spycraft does not remove romance from life. It keeps your eyes open while romance is trying to close them.

Operation 4: The Bad Apology

Situation: Someone gives you an apology that sounds polished but changes nothing. The words are correct. The pattern remains intact. They may apologize quickly because they want the discomfort to end, not because they have understood the damage.

Field read: The useful question is not whether the apology sounded sincere. The useful question is whether the person accepts cost. A real repair changes behavior, absorbs inconvenience, and reduces the chance of repetition. A performance apology asks you to restore access without requiring adjustment.

Move: Acknowledge the words without surrendering the boundary. "I appreciate you saying that. I still need to see it handled differently." Keep the future behavior in view. Do not debate tone if the real problem is pattern. Do not let emotional relief substitute for evidence.

Debrief: Trust is rebuilt through deposits, not speeches. A person who wants the benefit of forgiveness without the discipline of repair is asking for access on credit.

Operation 5: The Public Confrontation

Situation: Someone confronts you in public. The crowd may be small, but the presence of observers changes the geometry. The other person may want resolution, but they may also want an audience. Your ego feels the invitation immediately.

Field read: Public confrontation introduces performance pressure. People often escalate because they do not want to look weak. That means the crowd has become a third participant even if nobody else speaks. Your priority is not winning the spectators. It is protecting freedom of action, safety, and later options.

Move: Lower the volume. Slow the pace. If the issue is legitimate, move it to a private or controlled setting. "We are not handling this here." If the person wants spectacle, deny it calmly. If there is danger, create distance and move toward help, employees, security, or exit routes. Do not let pride pin your feet to bad ground.

Debrief: Public drama is a position trap. Once you accept the stage, every move is shaped by the audience. The cleanest win may be refusing the theater.

OPERATION 6: THE SALES FRAME

Situation: A salesperson, recruiter, influencer, or persuasive friend creates urgency around a decision. The offer may be real. The pressure may still be dirty. Limited time, social proof, fear of missing out, authority language, and manufactured scarcity all narrow your field of view.

Field read: The issue is not whether the offer has value. The issue is whether the pressure is preventing assessment. Urgency can be legitimate, but manipulators use urgency to separate people from comparison, advice, and reflection.

Move: Reclaim time. Ask what changes if you decide tomorrow. Ask for the terms in writing. Ask what the downside is. A clean offer can tolerate clean questions. If the answer becomes more emotional as you ask for clarity, that tells you something.

Debrief: A rushed yes is often a captured yes. Good timing includes knowing when delay is the strongest move.

OPERATION 7: THE ONLINE PILE-ON

Situation: A social post, group chat, or online thread turns against a person, idea, company, public figure, or event. People begin repeating a frame faster than they verify facts. Outrage becomes a membership signal.

Field read: The emotional climate is doing the work. The group is not simply discussing information. It is sorting people into moral categories based on speed and intensity of response. The danger is being pushed into a statement before you know what is true or what purpose the outrage serves.

Move: Slow the feed. Ask what is confirmed, what is inferred, and who benefits from the current frame. Do not reward speed over accuracy. If you must speak, speak narrowly. "I do not have enough verified information yet." That sentence is unfashionable and often correct.

Debrief: Propaganda loves emotional deadlines. Intelligence work resists them. A calm person withholds judgment long enough for facts to arrive.

OPERATION 8: THE LATE-NIGHT DECISION

Situation: You are tired, irritated, hungry, or emotionally depleted, and a decision presents itself. It may be a message you want to send, a purchase you want to make, a confrontation you want to start, or a promise you want to offer just to end discomfort.

Field read: Fatigue changes the quality of judgment. It narrows the future and inflates the present. A problem that would be manageable at noon can feel like a verdict at midnight. Many expensive choices are not made by bad people. They are made by depleted people trying to escape a feeling.

Move: Build a delay rule. If the decision can wait until morning without real danger, let it wait. Draft the message and do not send it. Put the item in the cart and close the browser. Write the angry speech in a note and review it after sleep. Protect future freedom from current chemistry.

Debrief: Self-control is not always heroic. Sometimes it is simply refusing

to let your worst hour sign documents for
your better self.

PAPERBACK FIELD LOGS

These final pages are intentionally
practical. They are here because a
paperback can do something an ebook
cannot do as naturally: hold evidence of
use. Work these logs in pencil or pen.
Keep the answers short. The purpose is
repeated contact with the principles.

FIELD LOG 1: ONE SITUATION, ONE LESSON

Situation observed:

____

What changed first?

____

What did I notice too late?

____

What improved my position?

____

What made me reactive?

____

What will I practice next time?

____

Doctrine line:

____

_____

FIELD LOG 2: ONE SITUATION, ONE LESSON

Situation observed:

____

What changed first?

____

What did I notice too late?

____

What improved my position?

____

What made me reactive?

____

What will I practice next time?

____

Doctrine line:

____

_____

FIELD LOG 3: ONE SITUATION, ONE LESSON

Situation observed:

____

What changed first?

____

What did I notice too late?

____

What improved my position?

____

What made me reactive?

____

What will I practice next time?

____

Doctrine line:

____

______

FIELD LOG 4: ONE SITUATION, ONE LESSON

Situation observed:

____

What changed first?

____

What did I notice too late?

____

What improved my position?

____

What made me reactive?

____

What will I practice next time?

____

Doctrine line:

____

____

FIELD LOG 5: ONE SITUATION, ONE LESSON

Situation observed:

____

What changed first?

____

What did I notice too late?

____

What improved my position?

____

What made me reactive?

____

What will I practice next time?

____

Doctrine line:

____

____

FIELD LOG 6: ONE SITUATION, ONE LESSON

Situation observed:

____

What changed first?

____

What did I notice too late?

____

What improved my position?

____

What made me reactive?

____

What will I practice next time?

____

Doctrine line:

____

_____

FIELD LOG 7: ONE SITUATION, ONE LESSON

Situation observed:

____

What changed first?

____

What did I notice too late?

____

What improved my position?

____

What made me reactive?

____

What will I practice next time?

____

Doctrine line:

____

______

FIELD LOG 8: ONE SITUATION, ONE LESSON

Situation observed:

____

What changed first?

____

What did I notice too late?

____

What improved my position?

____

What made me reactive?

____

What will I practice next time?

____

Doctrine line:

____

______

FIELD LOG 9: ONE SITUATION, ONE LESSON

Situation observed:

____

What changed first?

____

What did I notice too late?

____

What improved my position?

____

What made me reactive?

____

What will I practice next time?

____

Doctrine line:

____

____

FIELD LOG 10: ONE SITUATION, ONE LESSON

Situation observed:

____

What changed first?

____

What did I notice too late?

____

What improved my position?

____

What made me reactive?

____

What will I practice next time?

____

Doctrine line:

____

____

FIELD LOG 11: ONE SITUATION, ONE LESSON

Situation observed:

____

What changed first?

____

What did I notice too late?

____

What improved my position?

____

What made me reactive?

____

What will I practice next time?

____

Doctrine line:

____

____

FIELD LOG 12: ONE SITUATION, ONE LESSON

Situation observed:

____

What changed first?
____

What did I notice too late?
____

What improved my position?
____

What made me reactive?
____

What will I practice next time?
____

Doctrine line:
____
____

FIELD LOG 13: ONE SITUATION, ONE LESSON

Situation observed:
____

What changed first?
____

What did I notice too late?
____

What improved my position?
____

What made me reactive?
____

What will I practice next time?
____

Doctrine line:

____

____

FIELD LOG 14: ONE SITUATION, ONE LESSON

Situation observed:

____

What changed first?

____

What did I notice too late?

____

What improved my position?

____

What made me reactive?

____

What will I practice next time?

____

Doctrine line:

____

____

FIELD LOG 15: ONE SITUATION, ONE LESSON

Situation observed:

____

What changed first?

____

What did I notice too late?

____

What improved my position?

____

What made me reactive?

____

What will I practice next time?

____

Doctrine line:

____

_____

FIELD LOG 16: ONE SITUATION, ONE LESSON

Situation observed:

____

What changed first?

____

What did I notice too late?

____

What improved my position?

____

What made me reactive?

____

What will I practice next time?

____

Doctrine line:

____

_____

Field Log 17: One Situation, One Lesson

Situation observed:

____

What changed first?

____

What did I notice too late?

____

What improved my position?

____

What made me reactive?

____

What will I practice next time?

____

Doctrine line:

____

_____

Paperback Debrief: What Changes After This Manual

A field manual has done its job when the reader becomes less dramatic and more capable. The work should not make you

louder. It should make you harder to
rush, harder to bait, and harder to steer
without your consent. If someone notices
the change at all, they should notice
steadiness before they notice technique.

The first change should be attention.
You should see rooms earlier, hear motive
sooner, and notice when a question is
really a request for access. You should
feel less need to answer every pressure
immediately. That small delay is not
hesitation. It is the space where
judgment returns.

The second change should be cleaner
language. Less explaining. Less arguing
with bad frames. More precise questions.
A better no. A better yes. A better
pause. Ordinary sentences become tools
when they are attached to intention
instead of reflex.

The third change should be position.
Choose better seats. Keep better exits.
Make better requests. Protect private
information with less guilt. Build trust
through reliability rather than
performance. Leave scenes before they
become traps. None of that requires
fantasy. It requires repetition.

This paperback is built to be used, not
admired from a shelf. Mark the field
logs. Run the drills. Return to the laws
when pressure makes you stupid, because
pressure makes everyone stupid unless
training has given them a route back to
useful behavior.

Conclusion: The Ordinary Edge

Spycraft is not about pretending to be someone else. It is about finally paying attention to the world you are already in.

The useful version is quieter than the fantasy version. It looks like remembering a name, noticing a doorway, delaying a bad answer, refusing an intrusive question, reading pressure in another person, and leaving before the room turns. None of that requires costume, drama, or permission.

The work is to become harder to move carelessly. Harder to deceive. Harder to rush. Harder to corner. Easier to trust. Easier to rely on. Better positioned when other people lose their heads.

That is the art and science of spycraft. Not romance about secret worlds, but practical control of attention, information, timing, position, and choice in the world you already occupy.

Instructor's Closing Note

I do not teach spycraft because I want ordinary people pretending to live in a secret world. I teach it because ordinary people already live inside pressure, persuasion, uncertainty, risk, and incomplete information. They already have to read people. They already have to protect privacy. They already have to decide whom to trust, when to speak, when to leave, and when to keep still.

The language of spycraft gives those ordinary decisions sharper handles. It does not make life theatrical. It makes the hidden parts of normal life easier to see. Access, motive, cover, timing, position, and information are not exotic ideas. They are the mechanics underneath everyday human behavior.

Use the material that proves itself. Drop anything that makes you perform. The best sign that the work is taking hold is not that you look more mysterious. It is that you become calmer, more observant, more reliable, harder to rush, and better positioned when the room changes.

That is enough. Quiet skill usually is.

ABOUT THE AUTHOR

P.J. Agness is the founder of Archangel Protective Intelligence. He teaches self-defense, protective intelligence, personal security, and practical spycraft for everyday life.

His work translates tradecraft, awareness, influence, and security concepts into clear tools ordinary people can use without fantasy or theatrics.